Heidi & Daniel Howarth

What Makes Me
Scared?

Sky Pony Press
New York

It was great having a big brother most of the time.
He was someone to play with, someone to annoy, and on very rare
occasions, someone to cuddle up with. Nothing could be better
than being snuggled up in a bundle of soft, warm fur.

But as all brothers, or even sisters, can be, he could also be very, very annoying!

"Look at you, scaredy cat!" called his brother. "You are such a wimp that one day I think you will actually scare your spots right off your back. You are too scared to be a proper leopard." But Little Leopard was proud of who he was, so he just ignored him. And secretly he wondered if his brother was scared of anything, too. If he was he never showed it.

Being the smallest in the family was always a challenge,
but there were some things that Little Leopard loved.
Little Leopard loved how fast he could run, even though
his brother would run faster.

"Come on!" he shouted. "You can go faster!
Are you a leopard or a sloth?" But Little Leopard couldn't.
Going too fast felt scary and just a little too unsafe.

Little Leopard loved how well
he could climb, even though
his brother could climb higher.

"Come on!" his brother teased. "Even a baby
elephant could climb trees better than you."
But Little Leopard couldn't.
The height made him dizzy.
And his tiny paws trembled.

Little Leopard loved swimming, even though
his brother could swim in deeper water.
"Come on!" he called. "Your paws are barely wet;
they are drier than a desert fox's."
His brother laughed and Little Leopard always
felt silly. But the truth was that deep down
he was just nervous.

When the wind blew late at night,
high in the trees he worried about
what would happen if the wind
blew harder and harder and
the tree came crashing down.
When the rain began to sprinkle
from the sky, Little Leopard
worried about what would happen
if the rain became
a storm and the storm flooded
the whole forest.
Little Leopard thought a lot and
worried a lot and the truth was
that his brother did not think
very much at all!

His dad was strong and brave, his big brother was tough, and deep down, Little Leopard was . . . scared! He hated being scared but he could not stop worrying. That night at bedtime he was still worried. But someone had noticed.

Mommy Leopard asked, "What's up? It is getting late.
Can't you sleep, little one?" She snuggled in close and
Little Leopard hugged her tight.
He was not sure if he should tell her what was wrong.
He felt a little bit silly. It was hard to explain and
he did not know where to begin.
"I'm fine," he said. Mommy just hugged him closer,
she knew he would tell her what was wrong eventually.
"You know you can talk to me about anything, don't you?"
she said in that very gentle way that only Mommy Leopard could.

That night Little Leopard worried as he lay awake and the more
he worried, the more he realized he was not just scared for
himself. What actually worried him more than anything was
the thought that anything could happen to his family.
In the morning he would talk to his mommy.
With that nice thought in his mind, he fell fast asleep.

Over breakfast, Little Leopard was still wondering where to start.
"Mommy," he whispered quietly.

He did not want his brother to hear.
"Do you ever get scared?"

At first Mommy did not seem to hear,
but when she turned around, it was clear
she was thinking.
"Let me see," she said.
"I am scared of a lot of things."
As she began to explain all the fears
she had Little Leopard found himself nodding.
The more she talked the more everything
made sense.

"You see, Little Leopard," she said, "the forest is a place of danger and it is in our nature to protect ourselves. The way we do this is by knowing when to stop. To look before we leap, to check the trail ahead. And I am very glad you take such good care of yourself, because there is only one thing that really scares me."

Little Leopard waited for her to continue.
"The only thing that really scares me is the thought of losing you . . . any of you."
And with that, Little Leopard realized they were not alone.

His dad smiled a reassuring smile and nodded his head.
"Yes," he agreed. "That scares me too."
Little Leopard's brother was there too, looking
a little embarrassed. "I'm sorry I pushed
you," he said. "I didn't want you to
be scared . . . like I was when
I was little!"

So they all spent that day together.
They climbed the trees, but to a safe height.
They played in the river, but stayed in the shallows.
And lastly, as the shadows were falling across the forest,
they climbed up to a comfy branch, and as night fell and
the darkness spread, Little Leopard was no longer afraid.
He was just full of wonder as the sky became speckled
with stars.

He dreamed a lot that night.
He dreamed of all the things
that had ever worried him.
But this dream was different.

In this dream he was strong and brave. In this dream he was a big, strong leopard as powerful as his dad. A brave leopard as adventurous as his brother. A clever leopard every bit as wonderful as his mommy.

It **could** scare your spots off

Before starting to share this story with children, look at the front cover and help them to read the title. Can the children guess what the story is about? Where do they think it takes place?

How do the children feel about some of the most common fears: spiders, the dark, water?

This story is about being small and being afraid. Little Leopard is not scared of everything, but he is a clever little kitten who worries about all the dangers that exist in the forest.

He is scared of the dark and scared of the wind when it blows through the trees, and having a very confident older brother does not do a lot to help him.

He teases him about his fears and plays tricks to scare him. Have the children ever been scared? What was it that worried them? Who would be the person in their family they could go and talk to about a concern or a fear? Who else could they talk to? Maybe a teacher.

It is perfectly natural for us to have fears; it is part of our heritage. As a leopard, Little Leopard needs to have certain fears; they are natural responses to the dangers in the forest and having them would be very good for his survival.

So some fears are sensible. They help us to make choices about our own safety, but other fears can be irrational.

A phobia is an irrational fear of something that is so strong that the person completely avoids the source of the fear. For example, some people have Vermiphobia. This is a fear of the common earthworm. Now this may seem silly to you or me, because what harm could a little worm do? They have no teeth or claws. But the fear can be so strong for some people that if it rains and there is a possibility of worms coming to the surface they never go outside.

Have the children ever heard the word "phobia"? Do they understand what that word means?

What Makes Me Scared?

First Sky Pony Press Edition 2019.

Sky Pony Press books may be purchased in bulk at special discounts for sales promotion, corporate gifts, fund-raising, or educational purposes. Special editions can also be created to specifications. For details, contact the Special Sales Department, Racehorse for Young Readers, 307 West 36th Street, 11th Floor, New York, NY 10018 or info@skyhorsepublishing.com.

Sky Pony® is a registered trademark of Skyhorse Publishing, Inc.®, a Delaware corporation.

Visit our website at www.skyhorsepublishing.com.

10 9 8 7 6 5 4 3 2 1

Author: Heidi Howarth
Illustrations: Daniel Howarth
Design and layout: Gemser Publications, S.L.
Cover design: Mona Lin

Library of Congress Cataloging-in-Publication Data is available on file.

Print ISBN: 978-1-5107-4550-6
Ebook ISBN: 978-1-5107-4564-3

Printed in China